The Spring Equinox

CELEBRATING THE GREENING OF THE EARTH

BY ELLEN JACKSON

ILLUSTRATED BY JAN DAVEY ELLIS

The Millbrook Press   Brookfield, Connecticut

For my father
E.J.

For my mother, E.D.
J.D.E

Library of Congress Cataloging-in-Publication Data
Jackson, Ellen B., 1943-
The spring equinox : celebrating the greening of the earth / Ellen Jackson;
illustrated by Jan Davey Ellis
p. cm.
Includes bibliographical references
ISBN 0-7613-1955-7 (lib. bdg.) 0-7613-1644-2 (trade)
1.Vernal equinox—Juvenile literature. 2. Spring festivals—Juvenile literature.
[1. Spring festivals. 2. Festivals. 3. Holidays.] I. Ellis, Jan Davey, ill. II. Title.
GT4995.V4 J32 2002
394.262—dc21   2001030435

Published by
The Millbrook Press, Inc.
2 Old New Milford Road
Brookfield, Connecticut 06804
www.millbrookpress.com

Printed in the United States of America
lib: 5 4 3 2 1
trade: 5 4 3 2 1

Have you ever wondered what causes the seasons? Scientists have shown that the seasons are caused by the tilt of the Earth's axis in relation to the sun.

When the Northern Hemisphere is tilted toward the sun, the northern part of the world receives more hours of sunlight and the people in the Northern Hemisphere experience summer. In the winter, the opposite is true. The Northern Hemisphere is tilted away from the sun and receives fewer hours of sunlight.

But on two days each year, the fall and spring equinoxes, day and night are of equal length. The Earth is tilted neither toward nor away from the sun. The word *equinox* comes from a Latin word that means "time of equal days and nights." The vernal, or spring, equinox occurs in the third week of March. This special day marks the beginning of spring in the Northern Hemisphere.

Spring is a happy, hopeful season in most parts of the world. Lemon-yellow daffodils and white and pink tulips push upward toward the sun. The woods are filled with the sweet smell of damp earth, and birds are busy building nests.

People today know that spring follows winter as surely as night follows day. But thousands of years ago, ancient people feared the winter months when food was scarce and the Earth seemed to be asleep. Everyone worried that the sun might slip beneath the horizon and never return. At the time of the spring equinox when the days lengthened and the sun grew stronger, people were relieved. They knew that the flowers would bloom again and the crops would grow once more.

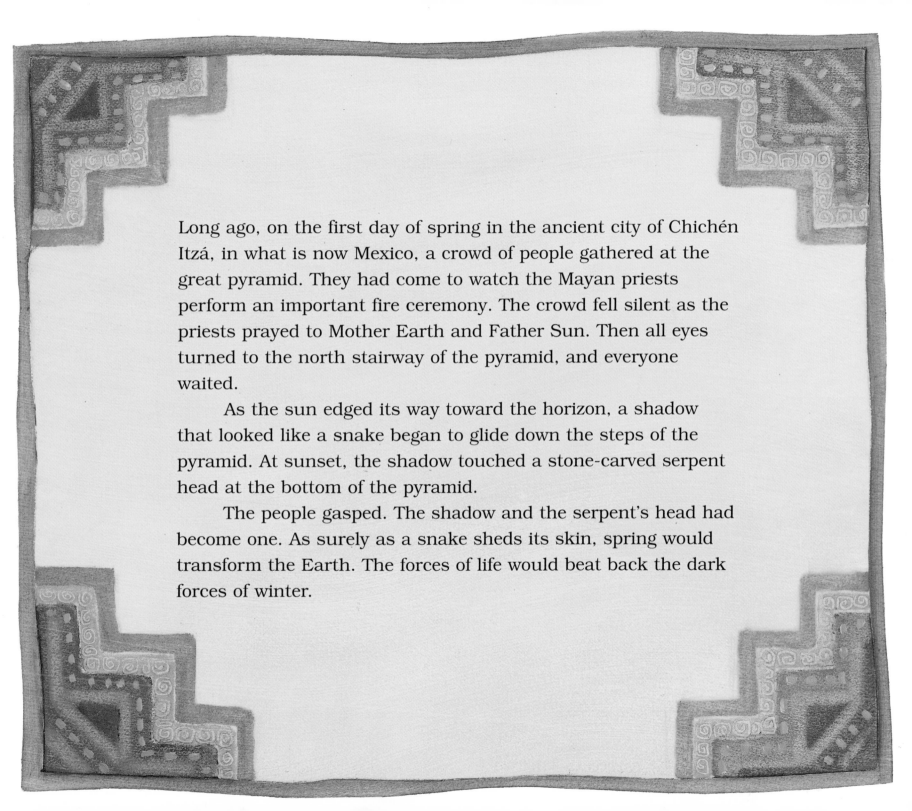

Long ago, on the first day of spring in the ancient city of Chichén Itzá, in what is now Mexico, a crowd of people gathered at the great pyramid. They had come to watch the Mayan priests perform an important fire ceremony. The crowd fell silent as the priests prayed to Mother Earth and Father Sun. Then all eyes turned to the north stairway of the pyramid, and everyone waited.

As the sun edged its way toward the horizon, a shadow that looked like a snake began to glide down the steps of the pyramid. At sunset, the shadow touched a stone-carved serpent head at the bottom of the pyramid.

The people gasped. The shadow and the serpent's head had become one. As surely as a snake sheds its skin, spring would transform the Earth. The forces of life would beat back the dark forces of winter.

Ancient peoples, such as the Mayans, believed that without special ceremonies the Earth would remain dead and barren. In many parts of the world, spring was a time for planting and sowing—and hard work. But the spring equinox was also a time of joy.

During the festival of Floralia in Rome, people celebrated the coming of spring with music and merriment. Roman children took part in the festival along with the adults. The children wound garlands of flowers around a marble column in a temple dedicated to Flora, goddess of flowering plants. Then they danced around the column singing songs of praise.

In Europe during the Middle Ages, people thought they needed to help the forces of spring conquer the forces of winter. Villagers gathered around bonfires, singing, dancing, and leaping through the flames. Dancers accompanied by jingling bells attempted to awaken the Earth. The dancers would leap as high as they could, hoping the grain would grow as tall as their leaps.

In some villages, a mock battle between summer and winter was acted out. Summer was represented by a man dressed in leaves and flowers. Summer would always defeat winter, which was represented by a man dressed in straw. In England, the fight between summer and winter became a football game between two teams. In other places, such as Ludlow in Shropshire, the battle was in the form of a tug-of-war with thousands of people taking part.

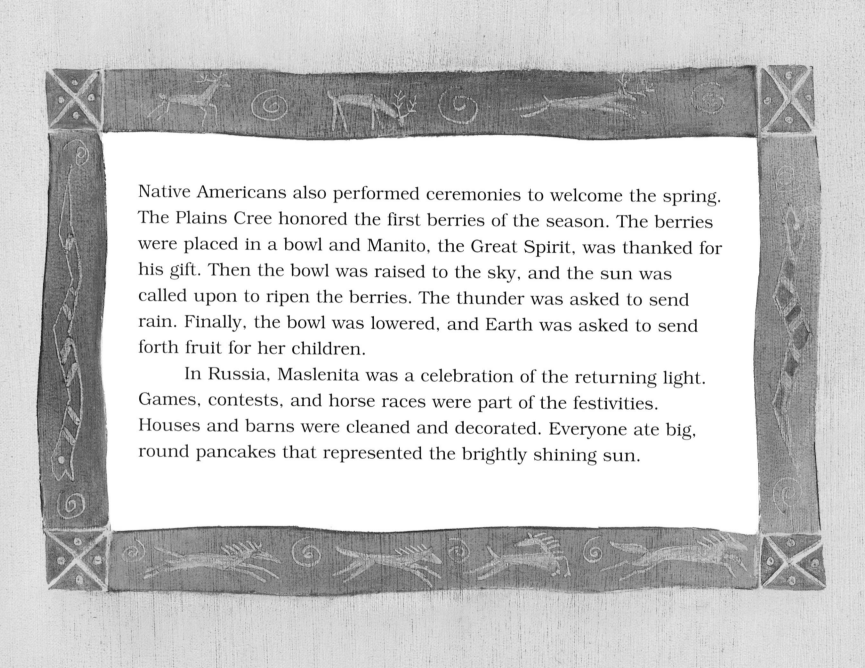

Native Americans also performed ceremonies to welcome the spring. The Plains Cree honored the first berries of the season. The berries were placed in a bowl and Manito, the Great Spirit, was thanked for his gift. Then the bowl was raised to the sky, and the sun was called upon to ripen the berries. The thunder was asked to send rain. Finally, the bowl was lowered, and Earth was asked to send forth fruit for her children.

In Russia, Maslenita was a celebration of the returning light. Games, contests, and horse races were part of the festivities. Houses and barns were cleaned and decorated. Everyone ate big, round pancakes that represented the brightly shining sun.

The Jewish holiday of Passover began as an ancient spring festival. Later it became a time to remember the flight of the Jews from slavery in Egypt.

Today, at the beginning of Passover, Jews prepare a special dinner called a Seder. At the Seder, the story of the Jews' escape from Egypt is retold. People sing Passover songs and eat special foods. The foods stand for different parts of the story. They include matzo, a dry bread made without yeast; a sweet mixture made from apples, nuts, honey, and wine; bitter herbs; and hard-boiled eggs dipped in salt water. The Passover story reminds everyone that joy can follow sorrow, and that winter will always be followed by spring.

In Iran, the thirteen-day Iranian festival of No Ruz begins the week before the spring equinox. No Ruz, which means "New Day," is a time of hope and renewal. Houses are cleaned, furniture is repaired, and fresh flowers are brought indoors. Cookies and sweets are presented to the older members of the family. Children receive coins or cash.

The day of the spring equinox is also the first day of the Iranian New Year. Each family celebrates the New Year by preparing a special table. Seven items that begin with the letter "S" in the Persian language are placed on the table. These items represent happiness and good fortune for the New Year. It is considered bad luck to remain at home on the thirteenth day of No Ruz. Almost everyone spends the day outdoors, enjoying a picnic with family and friends.

Holi is a joyous Indian holiday that comes at the end of winter. Holi is also known as the festival of colors. On this holiday, people run through the streets smearing strangers and friends with colored powder and dousing each other with colored water. At the end of the day, everyone is decked out in all the colors of the rainbow.

When Christians think of the spring, they are reminded of the Resurrection of Jesus. Easter, the holiday that commemorates the Resurrection, is held on the first Sunday after the first full moon after the spring equinox. On Easter, people gather in churches or beside lakes, streams, and oceans for special sunrise services. Easter eggs are dyed in beautiful colors, and people give Easter baskets to one another.

Many Easter customs come from the Old World. Eggs have always seemed magical and mysterious to people. An egg is a hard, unmoving object. But with a crack, a tiny, live creature can emerge from it. Eggs were honored, decorated, dyed, and exchanged by many ancient peoples.

Like the egg, the rabbit is a sign of springtime and fertility—probably because rabbits are especially active in the spring and produce many young at that time. It was the custom in Germany for children to build a nest in a field or garden in which the Easter Hare would lay its colored eggs. When German immigrants settled in North America, they brought this custom with them.

Some parts of the world do not experience seasonal changes in the weather. Even in these places, people celebrate the fertility of the Earth at special times of the year. The Bambara of Mali in Africa are farmers who work hard to grow millet, rice, and peanuts for their families. At planting time, men wearing male and female antelope headdresses perform a special dance. The dancers bend their heads as if to scoop up the earth with their horns. The purpose of this ancient dance is to honor and encourage the farmers who hoe the fields.

Not all spring holidays celebrated today have ancient origins. In 1969, former Senator Gaylord Nelson of Wisconsin decided that a special day was needed to remind people to protect the environment. On April 22, 1970, the first Earth Day was held. Earth Day helps us remember to love and care for the Earth and our fellow creatures. It is celebrated in the spring, a time when the precious beauty of the Earth is most apparent.

The spring equinox is a time of beauty—and it is also a time of balance. It is not quite summer yet, but not really winter anymore, either. It is a time when the world stands between the two seasons. It is a time to walk in balance with nature and look to the future.

A Spring Story

Easter may have been named for the Anglo-Saxon goddess of the dawn and springtime, Eostre or Ostara. Not much is known about this goddess. One legend says that she was always accompanied by a magical hare who could lay eggs. The following story is adapted from a myth about this goddess.

Long ago when the world was young, Ostara, the goddess of spring, walked across the land. As she walked, green and growing things sprung from her footsteps. Ostara seated herself on a rock, and a group of children gathered around her.

Ostara loved to make the children happy. She touched a rose bush, and it bloomed. Then she snapped her fingers. A cloud of butterflies appeared out of nowhere.

The children laughed and clapped their hands.

"Look! Look!" cried a boy. He pointed to something brown in the grass. There beside the child was a bird. Her wings had frozen in the last snowstorm of winter, and she was dying.

"Oh!" cried all the children. "It is so sad. Can you help her?"

"I will try," said Ostara.

Ostara cupped the bird in her hands. When she opened them, the bird had turned into a healthy rabbit. The children jumped up and down for joy.

But when the children looked at the rabbit, they saw that her face was full of sorrow.

The rabbit knew she could no longer sing. She could no longer lay eggs. And she could no longer fly above the clouds to escape her enemies. She was afraid. Two big tears rolled down her furry face.

"Change her back!" cried the children. "She doesn't want to be a rabbit. Let her be a bird again."

"It cannot be undone," said Ostara. "That is the way of magic. But I will give the rabbit a gift. On the first day of spring each year, she will lay her eggs. Then she will bring them to all the children of the world–for it was the children who saved her."

"What if a fox catches her?" asked a little girl. "She cannot fly."

"No fox will catch her. She will sail across the sky. For most of the year, the rabbit will live on the moon and be happy and safe from her enemies."

And so it was. Even today, if you look up at the sky you may see the rabbit in the moon. And if you listen with the heart of a child, you will hear a faint, rabbity song wafted on the breeze from far, far away.

** Author's Note: The story of Ostara was adapted from *The New Patterns in the Sky: Myths and Legends of the Stars* by Julius D. W. Staal.

 Spring Activities

BULGARIAN EGG GAME

In Bulgaria and other parts of Europe, children play this game with leftover Easter eggs:

You will need:
one hard-boiled egg for each child
basket for the eggs
mayonnaise
bread

1. Put all the hard-boiled eggs in a basket, and let two children select one egg each.
2. The two children tap their eggs together until one cracks. The winner is the child with the stronger egg.
3. Another child selects an egg and taps against the winner's egg until one cracks. The game continues with each child challenging the winner of the last round, until only one egg remains unbroken.
4. Remove the shells, and chop up all the eggs. Mix with mayonnaise and spread on bread to make egg salad sandwiches.

TISSUE-PAPER EGGS

Eggs have been dyed, painted, and decorated for thousands of years. Here is an easy way to dye eggs.

You will need:
Hard-boiled eggs
brightly colored tissue paper
bowl
scissors

1. Pour water into the bowl.
2. Cut the tissue paper into small pieces with the scissors.
3. Wet the tissue paper in the bowl.
4. Wrap an egg tightly with different colors of tissue paper. Squeeze out excess moisture. Leave the tissue paper on the egg for at least an hour.
5. Unwrap the egg.

PASSOVER MATZO

When the Jews were preparing to escape from Egypt, they had no time to wait for the bread to rise. Instead, they made bread without yeast, which doesn't need to rise. This recipe makes matzo, or unleavened bread, similar to that eaten by Jews at Passover to commemorate this event.

You will need:
1/2 cup (120 ml) all-purpose flour
1/2 cup (120 ml) whole-wheat flour
1/3 cup (80 ml) water, approximate
rolling pin
nonstick cookie sheet
fork

1. Preheat oven to 400°F (205°C).
2. Mix the two kinds of flour together.
3. Add the water one tablespoon at a time, kneading the dough between each tablespoon until the dough holds together in a ball. Knead the dough about 2 minutes longer.
4. Form little balls from the dough about 1 inch (2.5 cm) in diameter. Roll out each ball of dough until it is flat and very thin.
5. Make holes in each piece of dough with a fork.
6. Place on the cookie sheet and bake until slightly brown, 7 to 10 minutes.

IRANIAN NEW YEAR FEAST

Iranians celebrate the festival of No Ruz on the first day of spring. One way to mark this special day is with a special feast.

You will need:

seven foods that begin with the letter "S" (salad, sandwiches, salami, soup, sweet potatoes, strawberries, spinach, etc.)
candle
colored eggs
a bowl of water with one green leaf floating in it
tablecloth

1. Place the colored eggs, candle, and bowl of water on the tablecloth. How do these objects represent hope and new life?
2. Sample each of the seven foods. Enjoy!

JAPANESE BUTTERFLY

Origami is an ancient Japanese art. An origami animal, bird, or insect is made from a single square of paper that is folded in different ways. You can make an origami butterfly by following the instructions below.

You will need:

a square of pastel-colored construction paper
another piece of construction paper (same color)
colored pens or crayons
scissors
paste or glue

1. Fold the square of construction paper in half diagonally to form triangle A.
2. Fold triangle A in half to form triangle B. Then unfold triangle B.
3. Fold each side of triangle A up over the center crease at a right angle. Unfold.
4. The three creases in the center form the body of the butterfly. Use the pens to color the body at the center where the creases are.
5. Decorate the wings of the butterfly.
6. Cut a small oval out of the second piece of construction paper. This will be the head of the butterfly. Color the head. Attach it to the body with glue or paste.
7. Cut two small strips of paper and fold accordion style. These are the antennae. Color and attach to the head with glue or paste.

Bibliography

Barth, Edith. *Lilies, Rabbits and Painted Eggs: The Story of the Easter Symbols.* Topeka, KS: Econo-Clad Books, 1999.

Epstein, Sam, and Beryl Epstein. *European Folk Festivals.* Champaign, IL: Garrard Publishing Company, 1968.

Helfman, Elizabeth S. *Celebrating Nature: Rites and Ceremonies Around the World.* New York: The Seabury Press, 1969.

James, Edwin Oliver. *Seasonal Feasts and Festivals.* New York: Barnes and Noble, Inc., 1963.

Mandelbaum, David G. *The Plains Cree: An Ethnographic, Historical, and Comparative Study.* Saskatchewan, Canada: University of Regina, 1979.

Pegg, Bob. *Rites and Riots: Folk Customs of Britain and Europe.* Dorset, UK: Blandford Press, 1981.

Rosen, Mike. *Spring Festivals.* New York: The Bookwright Press, 1991.

Staal, Julius D. W. *The New Patterns in the Sky: Myths and Legends of the Stars.* Blacksburg, VA: The McDonald and Woodward Publishing Company, 1988.

About the Author and Illustrator

Author Ellen Jackson has written more than forty fiction and nonfiction books for children. Her best-selling *Cinder Edna* has won many awards, as has *Brown Cow, Green Grass, Yellow Mellow Sun*. A former elementary school teacher who now writes full-time, she lives in Santa Barbara, California, where she enjoys exploring tide pools along the shore.

Columbus, Ohio, artist Jan Davey Ellis has illustrated many successful books for Millbrook. Among the most recent are *The Quilt Block History of Pioneer Days With Projects Kids Can Make* and *A Sampler View of Colonial Life With Projects Kids Can Make*, both by Mary Cobb, and *Hasty Pudding, Johnnycakes, and Other Good Stuff: Cooking in Colonial America* by Loretta Ichord.

The author and artist together have created *The Summer Solstice, The Autumn Equinox,* and *The Winter Solstice*, which was a Children's Choice selection of the International Reading Association/Children's Book Council. Their collaboration, *Turn of the Century,* received a starred review from Booklist and a pointered review from Kirkus.